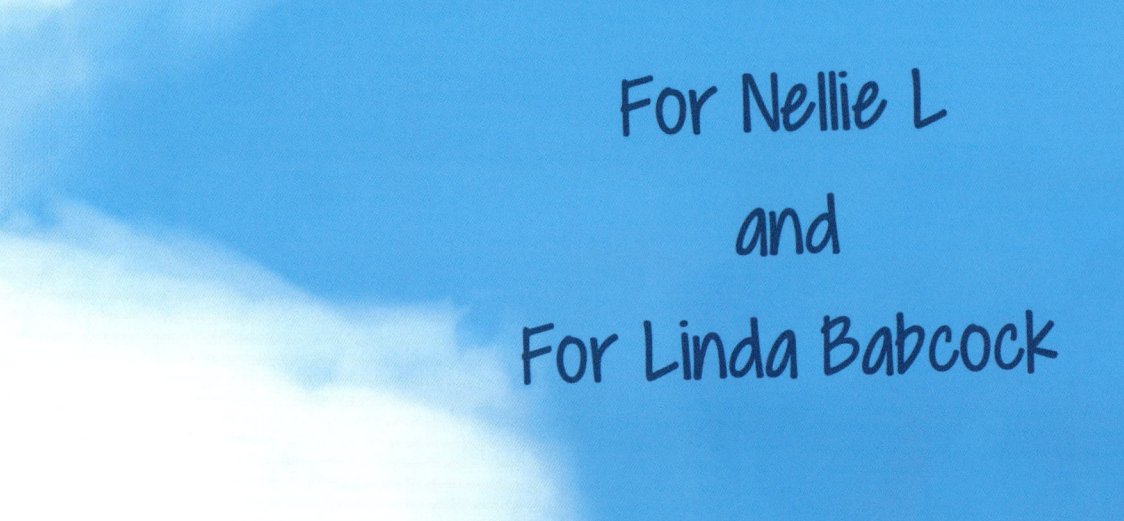

For Nellie L
and
For Linda Babcock

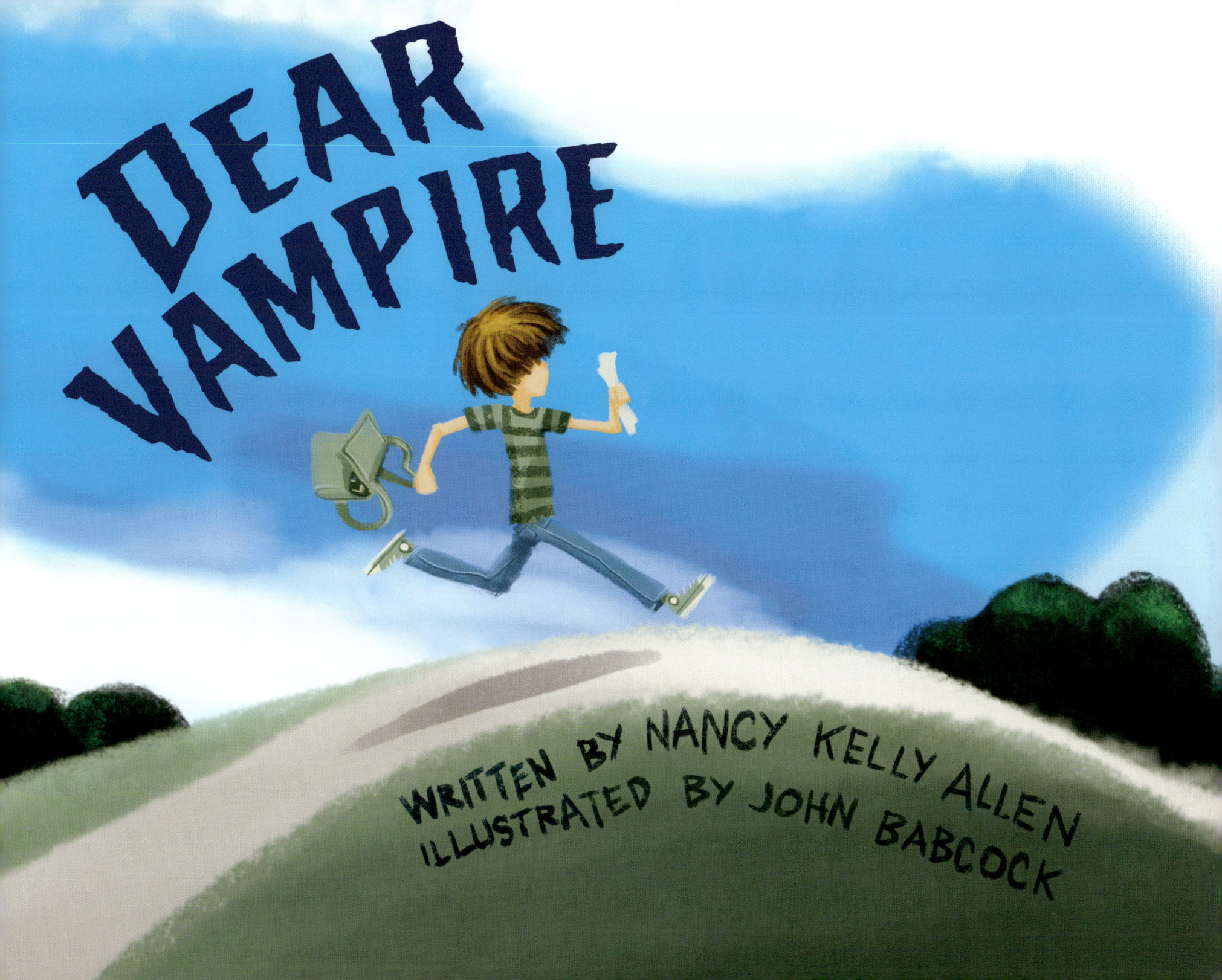

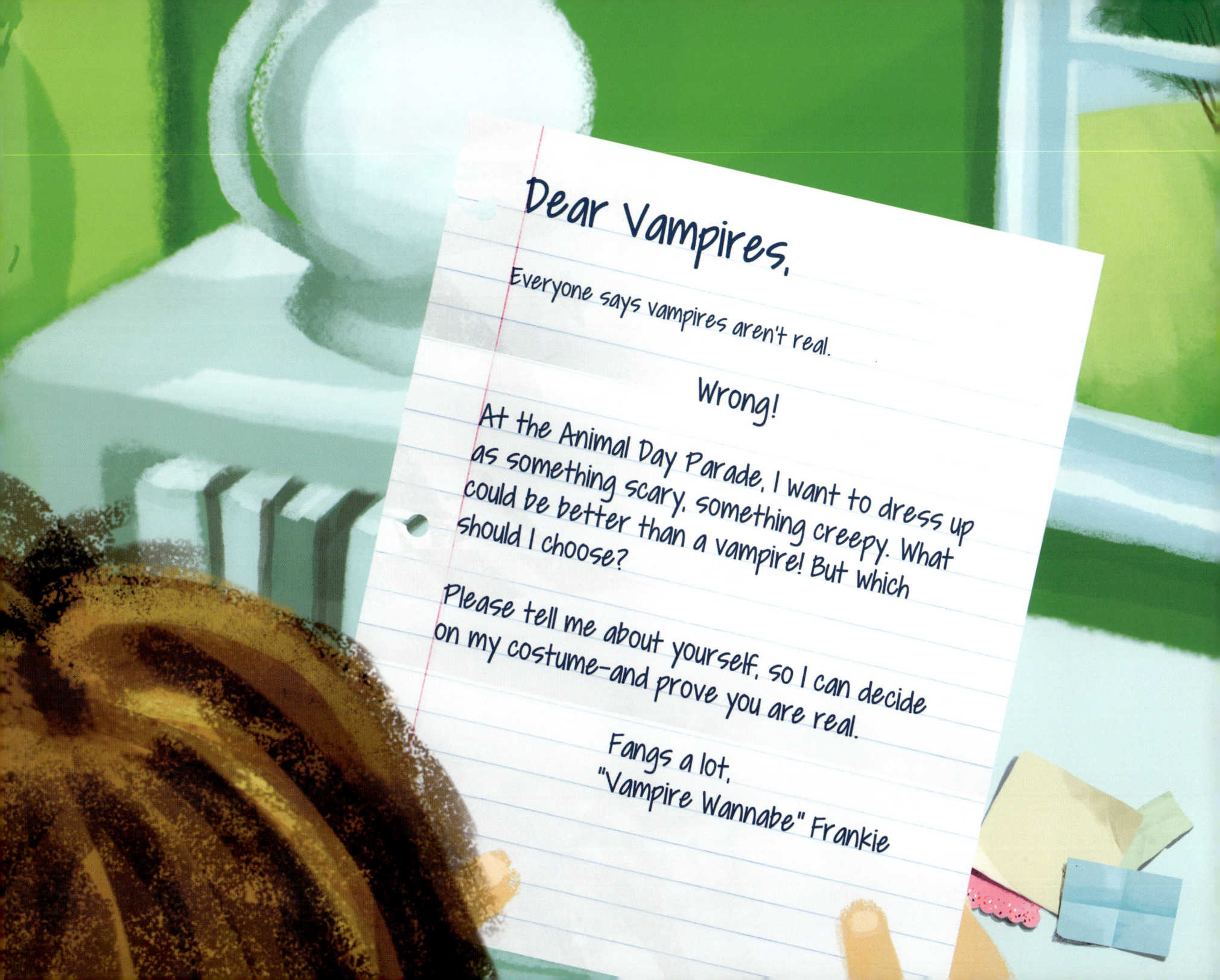

Dear Vampires,

Everyone says vampires aren't real.

Wrong!

At the Animal Day Parade, I want to dress up as something scary, something creepy. What could be better than a vampire! But which should I choose?

Please tell me about yourself, so I can decide on my costume—and prove you are real.

Fangs a lot,
"Vampire Wannabe" Frankie

Hey, VW,

Did you know mosquitoes-zzz are the most dangerous-zzz vampires-zzz to humans-zzz? That's right. Mosquitoes-zzz rank #1. We cause more human deaths-zzz than any animal on Earth. Sometimes-zzz our bites-zzz are deadly because we carry diseases-zzz. Malaria and yellow fever are two.

Have you ever been bitten by a vampire? Sure, you have. Female mosquitoes-zzz not only slice skin to suck blood, we spit into the wound, and that leaves-zzz you with an itchy, red bump. Sorry. Not!

Buzz-zzz-ing to bite,
Skeeter Mosquito

Mosquito is Spanish for "Little Fly"

MOSQUITO

IF A MOSQUITO BIT YOU, IT WAS A FEMALE. SHE NEEDS A BIT OF BLOOD TO LAY EGGS.

Mosquitoes are the world's deadliest animals. They carry diseases, such as malaria, yellow fever, and Zika virus, that kill people. But scientists believe mosquitoes should not be eliminated because they provide food for lots of animals.

Want to avoid mosquitoes? Go outside in the afternoon when temperatures are the hottest and insects are resting.

Dear Vamp,

No bones about it, I'm a worm—a lean, mean, cleaning machine. Teeth, I have plenty, about 300, razor sharp.

Sheesh! They don't call me "Sucker" for nothing. I've got two. One helps me move. The other drinks blo-o-o-o-o-d. People's blood. That can be a good thing. Some doctors use me to help patients who have blood clots. I break them up (not the people, the clots). Gotta go. Another patient waits. Lunchtime!

Where's the thanks?
"Ada Lott" Leech

LEECHES HAVE 32 BRAINS. THE WORM IS DIVIDED INTO 32 SECTIONS AND EACH PART HAS A SEGMENT OF A SINGLE BRAIN.

Leeches are everywhere! In every ocean and on every continent, except Antarctica.

If you're in water and a leech chooses your leg for dining out, just sprinkle a little salt on it. The leech will drop off soon.

Leeches are worms. Some are used for fish bait. Others are used as mini vacuums in hospital operating rooms to suction blood and increase blood flow in patients.

Listen Up, Wannabe,

I'm tired of getting a bad rap for being a bed bug. Sure, we hitch rides in grocery store bags and boxes to your abode. Sure, we hide out in cracks, behind doors, and in beds.

Sure, we chow down on your blood while you sleep. But you won't feel my bite, so what's the big deal, other than red welts? Toughen up.

Good night. Sleep tight,
"Bugsy" Bedbug

A BEDBUG'S SALIVA DEADENS THE PAIN OF THE BITE, SO PEOPLE DON'T WAKE UP WHEN BITTEN.

Their diet is the blood of warm-blooded animals, which includes people. These insects don't spread diseases, but their bites itch.

Bedbugs are the hitchhikers of the bug kingdom. They hitch a ride to places where they live — houses, office buildings, hotels, theaters, hospitals, schools, stores, and more.

They can live several months without a blood meal.

Want to be like me, Vam?

Daytime, I sleep. Nighttime, I drop from my roost, spread my wings, and fly. My stomach wants to go from empty to full as soon as possible. My super-smell-it nose knows when an animal is near.

I bite when the animals sleep. I only take a little blood so they almost never wake up.

Before I eat, flying is easy. I'm all fur and appetite. After I eat just one ounce, half my body weight, flying is HARD.

Guano happens
"Roy L. Pain" Bat

Bats are the only mammals that can fly. They live in colonies with hundreds of other bats in caves, mines, hollow trees, and old wells.

Vampire bats find food by using echolocation (EH-koh-low-KAY-shun), high, sharp sounds that help them find dinner.

Back at home, female vampire bats regurgitate blood and feed other hungry bats, both adults and babies. They often feed new mothers for two weeks after the babies are born.

IN ONE YEAR, MY 100-BAT COLONY CAN DRINK OVER 100 GALLONS OF BLOOD. THAT IS AS MUCH AS YOU WOULD FIND IN 25 COWS. BAT SALIVA PREVENTS THE PREY'S BLOOD FROM CLOTTING, SO THE VAMPIRE CONTINUES TO EAT FOR 20 TO 30 MINUTES.

Kissing Bug
1909 Nests and Lairs
Warm Climates,
The Americas
66213

Greetings, Wannabe,

I love animals so much I want to kiss them.

Mwah!

Rumor has it that I'm not as sweet as my name — kissing bug — sounds. My kiss is really a bite, and I "kiss" humans around their mouths for a few drops of blood while they are sleeping.

Honey, you'd never call me a picky eater, because I also like to "kiss" raccoons, opossums, and wood rats. Bless their hearts!

Most of my kisses are harmless. You may have a little itching, a little swelling, but nothing to complain about… unless I pass along Chagas disease. I have to admit, that can be… the kiss of death.

Pucker up!

MwaaahhHHH!
"Sugar" Kissing Bug

Hello, Vampire W,

Because I'm long and narrow, some wise guy named me Toothpick Fish. I live in the Amazon River shadowing my next meal. Catfish! I taste them in the water that comes from their gills.

Faster than you can say "Winner! Winner! Catfish dinner!" I dart into the catfish's gills and sip their blood! A minute or two later, it's exit time. The catfish never sees me. It pays to be translucent (that's like invisible).

So long, sucker!

Slim and trim,
"Candi" Candiru

Toothpick fish are about as narrow as a toothpick.

CANDIRU ("CANDY ROO") AND VAMPIRE FISH ARE OTHER NAMES FOR THEM.

Toothpick fish are almost transparent.

TOOTHPICK FISH LIE IN THE DEEP WATERS OF THE AMAZON AND ORINOCO RIVERS. THEY FEED BY ENTERING THE GILLS OF LARGER CATFISH. AFTER FEEDING, THEY SINK BACK TO THE RIVER BOTTOM TO DIGEST THE BLOOD.

BURP!

What's up, V?

This cat comes sniffing around, all purr and no hiss. Me, I'm hanging on to the edge of a leaf. When the feline passes, I drop in and bite. I've been told I'm a pain in the neck. Some say we're going to the dogs, but we ticks like the blood of lots of animals. People, too. I'm a faithful vampire. Once I get attached to something, I stick with it.

I'm no artist, but I draw blood.

Tickled to gnaw you,
"Vein Drain" Tick

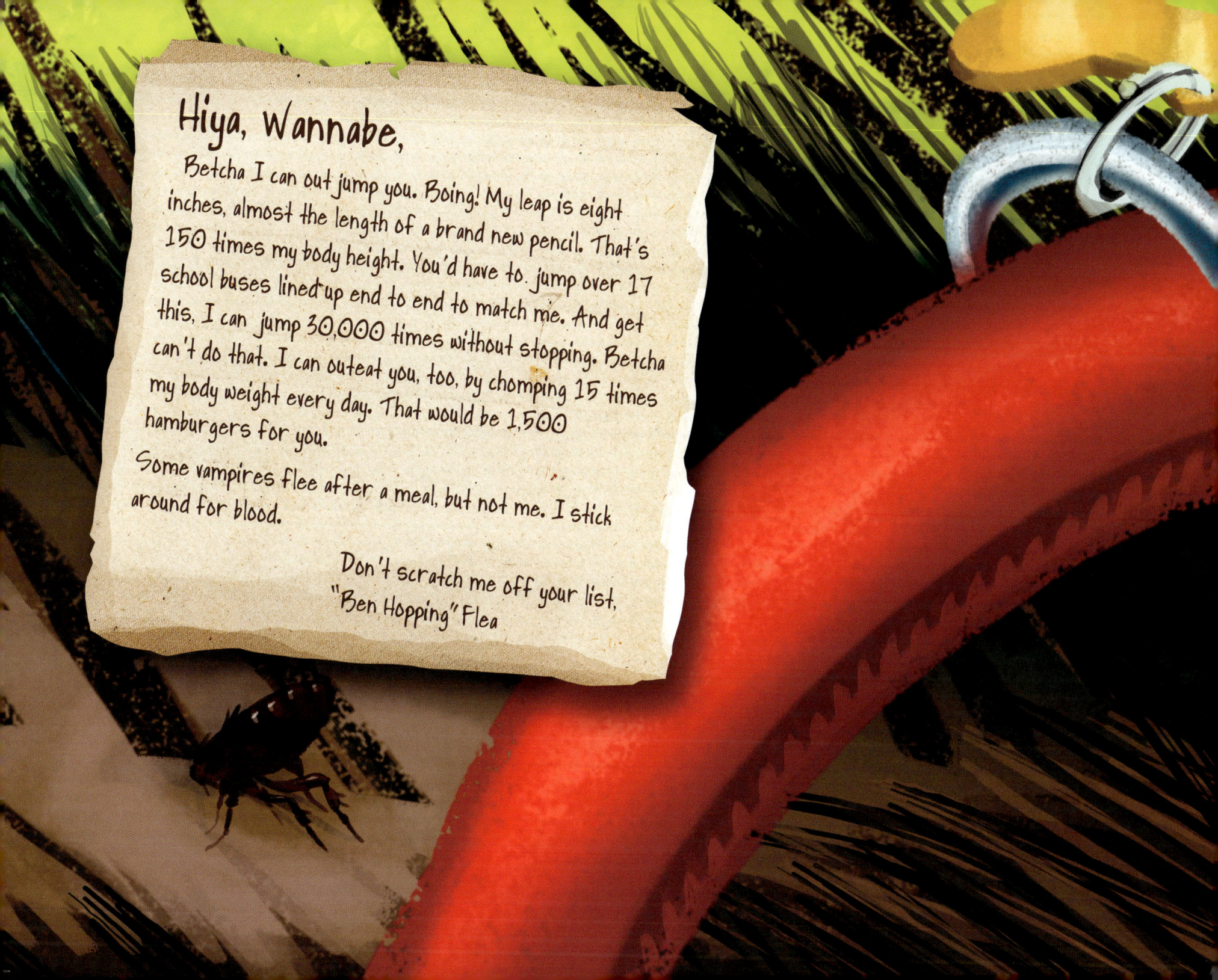

Hiya, Wannabe,

Betcha I can out jump you. Boing! My leap is eight inches, almost the length of a brand new pencil. That's 150 times my body height. You'd have to jump over 17 school buses lined up end to end to match me. And get this, I can jump 30,000 times without stopping. Betcha can't do that. I can outeat you, too, by chomping 15 times my body weight every day. That would be 1,500 hamburgers for you.

Some vampires flee after a meal, but not me. I stick around for blood.

Don't scratch me off your list,
"Ben Hopping" Flea

Dear Vampires,

Thanks for your letters. I knew you bloodsuckers were real! Real important, too. Each of you is part of nature's food chain. You dine on animal blood, and larger animals dine on you.

Unfortunately,

I can't choose between you so I'm not going to be any of you. I do have an idea though.

While I was poking around in the attic, I found different parts from lots of old costumes. I know I can put something together to be just the right animal, but I have to get more stamps. Thanks again.

A vampire believer,
"Frankie" Stein

Text copyright © 2022 by Nancy Kelly Allen

Illustrations copyright © 2022 by John Babcock

All rights reserved. No part of this book may be reproduced in any form without written permission from the publisher.

Library of Congress Cataloging-in-Publication Data available

ISBN 978-1-63333-057-3

Published by

www.thelittlefig.com